51 TIPS FOR ACADEMIC SUCCESS

COLLEGE EDITION

ALAN FARBER, PH.D.
LINDA O'BRIEN

WOODBURN PRESS

51 Tips for Academic Success
ISBN 978-0-9975890-1-6
Copyright 2016

Woodburn Press
405 Littell Ave.
Dayton, OH 45419
www.woodburnpress.com
888-285-1502

Introduction

Your college years are among the most formative and challenging years of your life. College offers many opportunities for personal and intellectual growth. It is a period of self-discovery, and a time for taking charge of your life.

Of course, first and foremost, you are attending college to pursue academic studies and prepare for a career—so succeeding in your classes must be your top priority.

This book will provide you with numerous tips, hints, and recommendations on how to make wise academic decisions, study effectively, and be successful in your classes.

College is an investment in your future. Have fun, work hard, and make the most of it!

"*Success is the sum of small efforts,
repeated day in and day out.*"

Robert Collier

TIP **1**

ATTEND
ALL
CLASSES

> *"If I could give freshmen one piece of
> advice, it would be to go to every class."*
>
> BRAD, MATH MAJOR

The importance of regular class attendance cannot be overemphasized.

When you skip classes, you miss out on lectures, notes, explanations of assignments, class discussions, tips on what may appear on exams, and changes to the syllabus.

Sure, it's tempting to miss a class now and then, particularly when you have an instructor who doesn't seem to notice whether or not you're there. But don't kid yourself into thinking that missing a class won't make a difference, or that skipping class now and then is okay as long as you get copies of the notes (which may or may not be any good).

There's also something else to consider—your grade may be partially based on your attendance. And even if it's not, a professor isn't likely to cut you any slack if you are often a "no show."

TIP **2**

SIT UP FRONT IN CLASS

"*I like sitting in the back, but I get more out of the class (and I get better grades) when I sit up front.*" MARIA, BUSINESS MAJOR

Arrive early on the first day of class and sit in one of the front three rows near the center.

This may become your permanent seat.

When you sit in the front, you're able to see what's written or displayed, and hear what's spoken. Plus you send a positive message to your professor—you're there to learn.

Students sitting up front seldom talk to one another, browse the web, text, chat, tweet, doze off, walk in late, or engage in other activities that are distracting and annoying. *Leave that to the back row crowd.*

TIP **3**

MAKE THE MOST OF YOUR STUDY TIME

"Do what you can, with what you have, where you are." THEODORE ROOSEVELT

51 Tips for Academic Success

As you have undoubtedly heard, you should be studying two (or more) hours for each hour in class.

But the key to success is not studying a lot, it's studying well.

- ▶ Combat fatigue by organizing your studying into 30-45 minute increments followed by 5-10 minute breaks.

- ▶ Before you start to study, make a plan. Decide exactly what you want to get done and the order in which you'll do it.

- ▶ Avoid marathon cramming sessions and all-nighters.

- ▶ Prepare for exams over the course of several days, rather than the night before.

- ▶ Study the hardest material when you're the freshest and most alert.

- ▶ Take advantage of extra-help sessions.

- ▶ If you find group learning to be beneficial, participate in study partnerships or study groups.

TIP 4

MEET WITH YOUR ACADEMIC ADVISOR

"You are never strong enough that you don't need help." CÉSAR CHÁVEZ

Your Academic Advisor can assist you with course selection, graduation requirements, and program planning. Make use of this valuable resource!

Schedule an appointment with your Academic Advisor early each semester. When you meet with your Advisor, bring a hard copy of your online degree audit (e.g., DARS, CAPPS) and a printed list of any questions you have regarding the following:

- ▸ General Education requirements
- ▸ Requirements for your major
- ▸ Prerequisites
- ▸ Electives
- ▸ Courses required for graduate or professional school admission
- ▸ Taking courses Pass/Fail, online, or during the summer (or intersession)

You may also want to ask your Advisor about withdrawing from courses, retaking courses, or studying abroad.

TIP **5**

COMPLETE ASSIGNMENTS EARLY

"Never leave til tomorrow that which you can do today." BENJAMIN FRANKLIN

Are you one of those people who set their clocks a little ahead to avoid being late? Good idea! Do the same with assignments.

Make it a practice to finish your assignments days before they're due.

This allows you time to review and revise your work, get input from others, and avoid silly last minute mistakes.

The same applies to applications for on-campus jobs, internships, scholarships and the like. Write and review all of these long before they are due.

Panic-driven, 11th hour work tends to be shoddy. Don't just meet deadlines—beat deadlines.

TIP **6**

GET ENOUGH SLEEP

"A good laugh and a long sleep are the two best cures for anything."

IRISH PROVERB

Success in college requires taking care of both mind and body.

Chronic fatigue (from insufficient sleep) contributes to illness and the inability to concentrate—which invariably results in academic underperformance. *You simply will not perform at your best if you are sleep deprived.*

Over-reliance on stimulants (in the form of caffeine, nicotine, over-the-counter drugs or illegal substances) will never substitute for a good night's sleep.

Combine getting enough sleep with a regimen of healthy eating and regular exercise and you will feel better, look better, and perform better.

TIP **7**

ALWAYS
FOLLOW
DIRECTIONS

*"Try assembling an IKEA dresser
without the instruction manual."*

DR. ALAN FARBER

Much of college success boils down to simply following directions.

You have a lot more autonomy and freedom in college. But like it or not, college life requires that you jump through quite a few hoops, *and that you pay close attention to instructions.*

For example, not following instructions such as these will most certainly result in lower grades:

- ▸ submit your report to your professor's email address before midnight

- ▸ write a three-page paper, double spaced, Times New Roman, 11 point font

- ▸ answer two of the three essay questions

You'll be amazed at how much success you'll have by simply following directions.

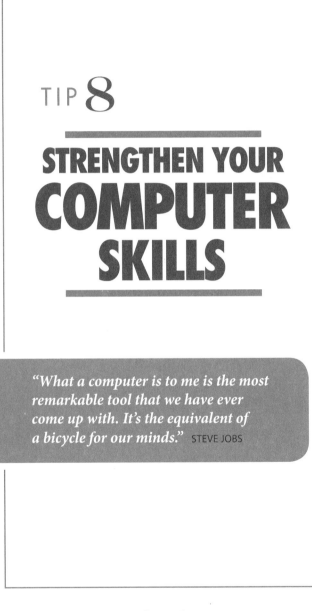

TIP 8

STRENGTHEN YOUR COMPUTER SKILLS

"What a computer is to me is the most remarkable tool that we have ever come up with. It's the equivalent of a bicycle for our minds." STEVE JOBS

You may not be a Computer Science major and you may never write a line of code, but you will be using computers throughout college and beyond.

Now is the time to learn the most popular programs (e.g., spreadsheets, graphic design, web development), as well as the programs used in your career field.

Microsoft Word is the standard in word processing. Familiarity with Word's shortcuts and special features will save you countless hours over the course of your college career.

To enhance your computer skills, check for computer courses and IT department workshops offered by your college, and visit Lynda.com for affordable online tutorials.

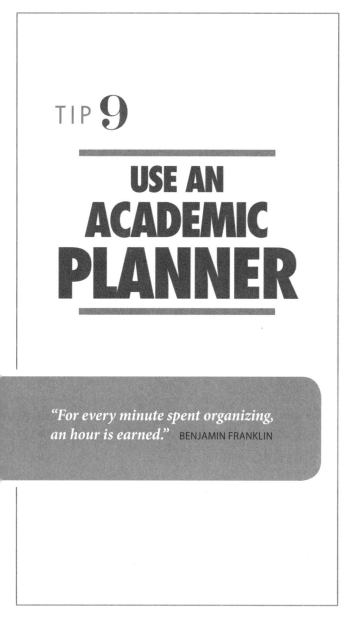

TIP **9**

USE AN ACADEMIC PLANNER

"For every minute spent organizing, an hour is earned." BENJAMIN FRANKLIN

In college, no one is there to remind you of what you need to do. You and your Academic Planner assume that role.

Keep your planner near you at all times, like a trusted friend. Write your name and phone number in it (in case it gets misplaced) and offer $10 for its return.

Pencil in class and study times, activities, appointments, events, and project deadlines.

Using a calendar on your phone or computer is fine, if you actually use it. Don't rely on your memory. Write everything down.

ACTIVELY
PARTICIPATE
IN CLASS

"If I zone out, a class can seem like it takes forever. When I participate, the time goes a lot faster." JOHN, ENGINEERING MAJOR

It's perfectly okay to spend time reading the newspaper, tweeting, texting, or napping. Just not during class.

You'll derive the most benefit from your educational investment by spending your time in class doing the following:

- ▸ listening
- ▸ taking notes
- ▸ asking for clarification
- ▸ responding to professors' questions
- ▸ offering your opinion

Your goal is not to impress your professor or classmates (although you certainly may), but to maximize your comprehension of the material.

To help ensure that you stay focused, put your phone away and stay off your laptop (unless it's being used with the professor's blessings in conjunction with the lecture).

TIP **11**

ENROLL IN
UNIV 101 / FIRST YEAR
COURSES

"I didn't think this course would be worth my time, but I'm glad I took it. I'll be a better student because of what I learned."
BROOKE, PHYSICS MAJOR

Colleges have a vested interest in the success of their incoming students and they've developed numerous programs to facilitate student success.

College success programs vary in length and go by a variety of names: *First Year Seminar*, *UNIV 101*, *Academic Strategies*, etc.

If this type of course or seminar is available at your college, enroll in it—even if it's not for credit. You'll learn how to navigate your college world, and you'll gain valuable skills.

Research shows that students who participate in "First Year" programs have higher GPAs and graduation rates than non-participants.

TIP **12**

USE
WAITING
TIMES

"If you want to make good use of your time, you've got to know what's most important and then give it all you've got." LEE IACOCCA

Time is a precious commodity in college, and successful students manage their time effectively.

"Waiting and wasted times" provide an opportunity to study, review notes, and catch up on reading.

Take advantage of snippets of time that may otherwise go wasted.

- ▸ the time between classes
- ▸ while doing your laundry
- ▸ waiting at a bus stop
- ▸ jogging on a treadmill
- ▸ while visiting a cafe

15 minutes here and 20 minutes there add up— and they free up time in the evenings for socializing and chilling out.

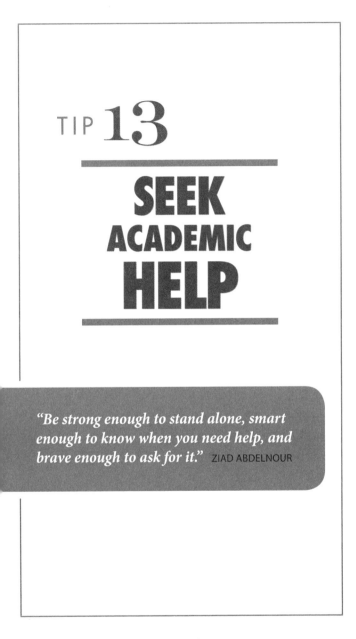

TIP **13**

SEEK ACADEMIC HELP

"Be strong enough to stand alone, smart enough to know when you need help, and brave enough to ask for it." ZIAD ABDELNOUR

College courses can be demanding and challenging, but there's lots of help available.

With so many people and resources to assist you in college, there's absolutely no reason to go it alone.

Reach out for help at the very first sign you may need assistance. Don't wait until it's too late to get extra help, or until your grade in a course is beyond improvement.

Check with your professor, TA (Teaching Assistant), and academic department about tutors, extra-help sessions, and campus Learning Centers (Writing, Math, Computer, and Study Skills Labs). Find a study partner, or look into joining a study group.

TIP 14

ACE THE EASY CLASSES

"*Whenever I have an elective, I look for a class that's interesting and fun. And I usually end up getting an A.*" SOPHIA, ECONOMICS MAJOR

There aren't many "cake" classes in college. But when you do encounter one—ace it.

Your GPA isn't weighted according to course difficulty—an A in *Organic Chemistry* (definitely not an easy course) affects your cumulative GPA the same as an A in *The American West in Cinema*.

You want to challenge yourself in college, but there's no shame in enrolling in the occasional less difficult elective class. *It'll help your GPA and perhaps free up some time to study for that Chemistry class.*

TIP **15**

ACTIVELY READ ASSIGNMENTS

"Reading is to the mind what exercise is to the body." JOSEPH ADDISON

To help you learn and remember what you read, preview the material, read with a purpose, and review.

Preview the material. Before you begin, read the introduction, section headings, and chapter summaries.

Read with a purpose. Before reading a section, think of a question that you want to answer—and don't proceed to the next section until you can answer your question.

Review. When you're finished reading, quickly go back over the assignment and restate the main points of each section.

Tip: Take notes as you read, and organize the main ideas into an outline—or use your notes to write a brief summary.

Don't bother trying to read when you're fatigued or distracted. Do your reading when you're alert and motivated to learn.

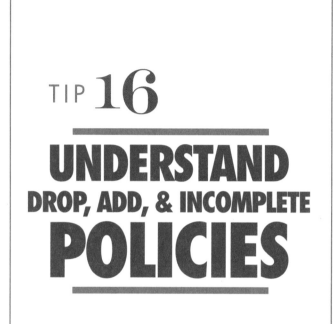

UNDERSTAND
DROP, ADD, & INCOMPLETE
POLICIES

"My math class was too hard for me, but when I went to drop it, I found out that I was too late. I was stuck." TJ, BOTANY MAJOR

The best time to learn these policies is long before you're considering a drop (withdraw), add, or incomplete.

Why? Because there are restrictions and deadlines that differ across departments and courses.

- ▶ If you withdraw after a certain deadline, you may lose some or all of your tuition.

- ▶ There are limits to the number of W's and I's you can have.

- ▶ A grade in a retaken course may either replace your initial grade or be averaged into your GPA.

And the list goes on. So before the semester begins, review your college's policies, and if you have questions, speak to your Academic Advisor.

Note: Even with a high GPA, a transcript full of W's and I's may hurt your prospects for graduate or professional school admission.

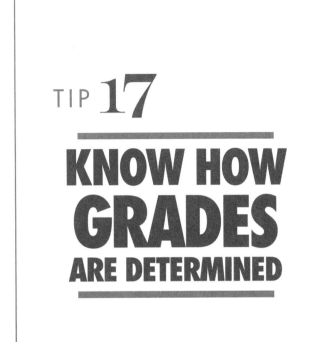

TIP 17

KNOW HOW GRADES ARE DETERMINED

"In my Lit class, I did fine on the tests, but because I missed some classes, I got a lower grade." STEVIE, ENGLISH MAJOR

Every course is graded differently.

The grading criteria may include exams, quizzes, assignments, group projects, lab reports, class attendance, presentations, class participation, and extra credit assignments. *(The latter is a no-brainer—always complete extra credit assignments.)*

Review the syllabus, identify how grades are determined, and devote your efforts accordingly. For example, don't spend 70% of your time on a project that only counts for 20% of your grade.

Do everything possible to keep up with assignments early in the semester. Playing catch-up becomes increasingly difficult as the semester progresses.

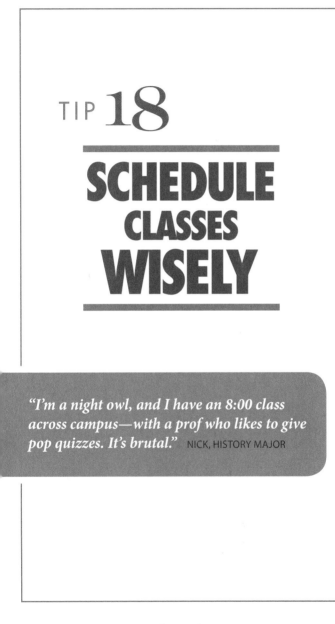

TIP 18

SCHEDULE
CLASSES
WISELY

"I'm a night owl, and I have an 8:00 class across campus—with a prof who likes to give pop quizzes. It's brutal." NICK, HISTORY MAJOR

Selecting the right courses is important—but so is the way your courses are scheduled.

Let's face it—most college students (especially freshmen) stay up way too late. So unless you're that rare breed of "morning person" who can function on fewer than six hours of sleep, avoid early morning classes.

The same applies to back-to-back classes. They make it harder to arrive early and stay late—giving you fewer opportunities to speak with professors and fellow students. This is especially true when classes are on opposite ends of the campus.

And you definitely don't want to be rushing from one class to another on exam days.

Whenever possible, space out your classes and use the time between them to review your notes, grab a bite, and prepare for the next class.

TIP **19**

BEFRIEND LIKE-MINDED STUDENTS

"You become who you hang around."

JEFF MILLER

The crowd you hang out with plays a major role in your adjustment to and success in college life.

Whether your school's enrollment is 1,000 or 30,000, you'll spend most of your time with a few dozen students during your college years. Select friends who share your values, interests, sense of humor, and commitment to academic success.

Make college an even richer experience by having an open mind and challenging yourself to meet people who are different from your regular social crowd.

One of the beauties of college is the opportunity to broaden your world view by meeting people from different cultures, ethnicities, and lifestyles.

TIP **20**

STRENGTHEN YOUR **WRITING** SKILLS

"The ability to express an idea is well nigh as important as the idea itself."

BERNARD BARUCH

College is writing-intensive, and the informality of texting and posting has hampered many students' academic writing.

If you feel that your academic writing skills could use improving, now is the time to take action.

- ▶ Enroll in a writing seminar and visit the college Writing Lab for assistance.

- ▶ Read a book or view online tutorials on basic grammar and writing rules.

- ▶ Visit "Grammar Girl" for helpful tips.

You are judged by your writing, whether it's exam essays and short-answer responses, internship and job cover letters, scholarship and graduate school applications, or social networking posts.

The key to writing a good paper is to make sure that you have enough time to plan, write, and revise it.

COME PREPARED FOR CLASS

"Before anything else, preparation is the key to success." ALEXANDER GRAHAM BELL

In college, you can't just study for exams—you need to prepare for each class by reviewing your notes and completing the assigned work.

When you come to class prepared, you get more out of the lecture, you know what the professor is talking about, and you're able to contribute to the class discussion. Preparing for each class also helps you keep up with the coursework—and it ensures that you don't fall behind in any of your classes.

To keep on top of things, constantly refer to the course syllabus. *And if you're covering Chapter 4 on Thursday, read Chapter 4 in advance.*

TIP **22**

SET
YOUR
PRIORITIES

"*Be assured that you'll always have time for the things you put first.*" LIANE STEELE

51 Tips for Academic Success

In college, it is easy to feel overwhelmed.

During a particular week, you may have a presentation to make, a 5-page paper and a group project due, a quiz, and an essay exam.

Deal with situations like this by drawing up a timeline that divides tasks into discrete, bite-sized components. Prioritize these tasks, taking into consideration due dates and the amount of work involved.

Reward yourself after you've completed a difficult task—stroll across campus, work out at the rec center, or call a friend. *Then move on to the next task.*

TIP **23**

REVIEW AND REVISE NOTES

"I've found that my notes usually contain most of what I need to know for the test." DARIUS, PSYCHOLOGY MAJOR

Take 10 minutes after class to go over your notes—while the information is still fresh in your mind.

Clarify anything that's confusing, highlight the important points, and put a question mark by anything you don't understand. Taking a few minutes to correct and edit your notes will make them much easier to study from later.

By reviewing and editing your notes, you're "locking" this information in your memory. Studies show that without review, almost half of what a person learns is forgotten in the first 20 minutes.

Editing and reviewing are the most important parts of notetaking!

TIP **24**

MANAGE TEST ANXIETY

"Always remember, you are braver than you believe, stronger than you seem, and smarter than you think." CHRISTOPHER ROBIN

All students experience some degree of test anxiety. It's normal.

Good study practices and thorough test preparation are the best antidotes for test anxiety.

If test anxiety is interfering with your test performance, try the following:

▸ Replace irrational thoughts (*I have to ace this test*) and negative thoughts (*I'll never pass this exam*) with thoughts that are realistic and positive (*I've studied hard. I'll do fine*).

▸ Reduce physical symptoms of stress (e.g., muscle tension, rapid heartbeat) with deep breathing, meditation, and exercise.

▸ Get a good night's sleep, have a healthy breakfast, and arrive to class a few minutes early.

Health & Wellness and Counseling Centers can offer additional tips for combating test anxiety.

TIP **25**

BACK UP ALL COMPUTER FILES

> *"Information is eternal, computers are ephemeral, backup is the savior."*
> WILLIAM R. STANEK

Computers can crash, be lost or stolen. Hard drives fail.

Every student's worst nightmare is lost or corrupted assignments, papers, or projects. When your 10-page assignment disappears, telling your professor that your computer crashed simply won't cut it.

Play it safe and create a back-up system. Save your files on a free cloud system like Google Docs, Media File, or Drop Box—or purchase an online backup system like Carbonite, iDrive or Mozy. External hard drives and USB sticks are fine, but they too can be lost, stolen, or corrupted. At the very least—email all documents to yourself as attachments, and save them to an email folder entitled "Important Documents."

When you spill coffee on your laptop, or your device mysteriously disappears from your room, you'll be glad you created a back-up system!

TIP **26**

USE LIBRARY RESOURCES

"A university is just a group of buildings gathered around a library." SHELBY FOOTE

51 Tips for Academic Success

Your college library offers more than your typical high school or public library. Take advantage of all it has to offer.

- ▶ Check your library's website for student orientation sessions.

- ▶ Learn about inter-library loans, online databases, and reference sites.

- ▶ Find quiet areas in the library that are conducive to uninterrupted study.

- ▶ Get to know the Reference Librarians. They'll offer suggestions for resources you'd never find on your own (or didn't even know to look for).

ARRIVE
TO CLASS
EARLY

"Better three hours too soon than a minute too late." SHAKESPEARE

51 Tips for Academic Success

Make a practice of arriving to class a few minutes early.

When you get to class early, you're more relaxed, and you have time to talk to classmates, check the syllabus, or review your notes.

Walking in late is not only rude, it sends the wrong message to your professor. Plus you'll miss announcements and introductory remarks.

And don't leave class early. Professors often summarize the lecture or discuss future assignments or exams at the end of class. And you may be able to catch your professor with any questions before he/she leaves. If it's a small class and you absolutely must leave early, inform the professor before class begins.

TIP **28**

JUST
SAY
NO

"We are created by the choices we make every day." BERNIE SIEGEL

There's plenty of opportunity for fun and games at college, but...

There will be times when you'll simply have to turn down invitations and requests to go places and do things.

Of course you want to be liked and accepted, but not at the expense of your academic success or personal integrity. "Just saying no" is all about behaving in accordance with your values, being true to yourself, and keeping your priorities in order.

True friends will understand that sometimes you have to hit the books, or just get some rest.

TIP 29

UNDERSTAND COURSE REGISTRATION

"Registration can be a jungle. Know your registration eligibility date and register as early as possible." YVONNE BAKER, REGISTRAR

These tips will help ensure that you get the classes you want.

▸ Schedule an appointment with your Academic Advisor months in advance to discuss course selection. Don't wait until the last minute when Advisors are swamped. *And have a list of questions ready.*

▸ Review the course catalog and create a list of first-choice classes, along with a list of alternate course selections.

▸ Get core requirements completed as early as possible.

▸ Schedule a good mix of classes. Don't overload yourself with difficult classes.

▸ Clear up any holds on your account before registration.

▸ If wait-listed, plead your case with the professor in person during his/her office hours.

Talk to a few juniors and seniors—they're bound to have some additional registration tips and advice.

TIP **30**

PARTICIPATE IN STUDY GROUPS

"Most great learning happens in groups. Collaboration is the stuff of growth."

SIR KEN ROBINSON

Study groups provide a forum for questions, explanations, clarifications, and study tips in a non-threatening and supportive environment.

When looking for a study group, avoid groups where all the members are struggling. You want a motivated, academically-oriented group that will challenge itself.

If there is no study group available, take the initiative to form one yourself. Ask your professor if you can make an announcement in class or pass around a sign-up sheet.

Limit your group to 4-6 members. Reserve a room somewhere quiet, bring snacks, create a study agenda, and have at it.

SCOUT OUT NEXT SEMESTER'S CLASSES

"Before everything else, getting ready is the secret of success." HENRY FORD

Be a wise consumer.

If you have questions or concerns about a course you're considering, check it out by doing the following:

▶ Speak to currently or previously enrolled students.

▶ Review the class syllabus.

▶ Leaf through the textbook at the bookstore.

▶ Sit in on a class. (You may need to get permission, or you might be able to simply walk into the lecture hall and take a seat.)

▶ Review teacher ratings on RateMyProfessor.

▶ Visit the professor during office hours to discuss the class—and note the vibe you get. If several sections of a course are offered, determine which professor and class time works best for you.

Meet with your Academic Advisor months in advance to plan next semester's course load.

TIP **32**

STUDY IN A
QUIET
PLACE

"Work hard in silence. Let success be your noise." FRANK OCEAN

Locate one or more quiet, well-lit, distraction-free spaces where all you can do is study.

Avoid friends, TV, music, non-academic web browsing—and mute your cell phone. By eliminating all distractions, you force yourself to do one thing only—study.

Scope out residence hall study lounges, the library, and unoccupied classrooms. For a change of pace, consider off-campus locations such as bookstores, coffee shops, or public libraries. For most students, the absolute worst place to study is their dorm room or apartment.

If your college has a law, medical, or other professional school library, check it out. They're quieter than undergraduate libraries, which makes them great places to study.

TIP **33**

UNDERSTAND ACADEMIC POLICIES

"Claiming 'I didn't know' won't cut it in college." ROB KING, STUDENT SERVICES

Do yourself a big favor…
carefully review your college and department's academic policies.

Failure to do so can cost you time, money, and a lot of aggravation. Here is a partial list of things to check out:

- **Academic Requirements**
  General Education Requirements
  Undergraduate Degree Requirements
  Major and Minor Requirements

- **Academic Workload**
  Dropping under a certain number of credits may affect your scholarship or work-study eligibility, whereas exceeding a certain amount may require permission.

- **Articulation Agreements**
  Which courses will and will not transfer from other schools?

- **Double Majors, Double Degrees, and Eligibility for Honors Programs**

Visit the Academic Policies section on your college's website, and meet with your Academic Advisor with questions or concerns.

TIP **34**

GET TO KNOW YOUR PROFESSORS

"Developing positive relationships with faculty is one way you can directly influence the quality of your education." DR. ALAN FARBER

There is nothing a professor likes more than a student who is genuinely motivated and engaged in the classroom experience. Be that student!

Sit up front in class, make eye contact, and ask and answer questions. Visit your professors during office hours to introduce yourself, inquire about extra help, or request career guidance.

Address professors with Dr., Mr., or Ms. When writing emails, have a clear Subject Line and specify which class section you are in. Be polite and use proper grammar (no slang, abbreviations, or emojis).

And if you're enjoying a class, let the professor know. It will make his/her day.

TIP **35**

STAY BUSY
BUT NOT
OVERWHELMED

*"Success usually comes to those who
are too busy to be looking for it."*
HENRY DAVID THOREAU

There's a saying: "If you want something done, give it to a busy person."

Students with too much time on their hands tend to squander it with social networking, partying, online gaming, TV viewing, and other time killers that do nothing to contribute to their academic and personal goals.

It's better to have a full, but manageable slate of academic, social, and volunteer activities. Staying comfortably busy teaches important life skills in time management, multi-tasking, and prioritization.

Make time for rest and relaxation. Even the busiest person needs to find time to care for mind, body, and spirit.

STUDY
ACCORDING TO YOUR
LEARNING STYLE

"I record myself reading an assignment and then I listen to it while I'm walking to class." WHITNEY, FRENCH MAJOR

Savvy students know how they learn most effectively—and study accordingly.

Visual Learners rely on the written word, PowerPoints, and videos to comprehend lessons.

Auditory Learners record and replay lectures, listen to podcasts, and recite material aloud.

Tactile Learners take notes and create graphs, charts, and outlines.

Independent Learners work best alone, while **Group Learners** benefit from study partners and groups.

Early Birds study best in the morning, whereas **Night Owls** may prefer hitting the books after sundown.

Identify your Learning Style and create a plan of attack that plays to your learning strengths.

DETERMINE COURSE LOAD BASED ON DIFFICULTY

"*I've learned to space out my lab classes. One semester I took three lab classes and I literally had no free time.*" WILL, BIOLOGY MAJOR

Taking 15-hours a semester is typical, but some semesters you may want to take more or less than 15 hours.

When taking a particularly hard ("killer") class you may want to lighten your load, and catch up later with a summer or intersession course. Or you may decide to take more than 15 hours if you're enrolled in an easy ("cake") class.

Only overload your schedule when you're 100% confident that you'll be able to devote the time and effort necessary to excel in all of your classes.

Know the deadline for dropping a course without a penalty—just in case you've taken on too much.

TAKE ORGANIZED NOTES

"Taking notes helps keep me focused."
TYLER, POLITICAL SCIENCE MAJOR

Tests usually cover material that's been presented in class. It is, therefore, important to have good notes from which to study.

▸ Put the subject of your notes, the name of the class, the date, and the page number at the top of each page of notes.

▸ Write on only one side of the paper—you can then spread everything out face up when studying.

▸ When taking notes, leave an extra space between topics, and create an extra wide left hand margin for key words.

▸ As you listen to a lecture, write key words (main topics, names of people, places, events, etc.) in your left hand margin. *Key words will help you organize your thoughts— and make your notes easier to understand.*

▸ Underline or highlight the most important information.

TIP **39**

BE A GOOD GROUP MEMBER

"Alone we can do so little, together we can do so much." HELEN KELLER

College is first and foremost a social environment.

Living and working among a diverse group of fellow students is one of the biggest challenges and greatest joys of college life.

▸ Always pull your weight when working on team projects.

▸ Treat classmates and dorm residents the way you'd like to be treated.

▸ Join student organizations and volunteer for committees, group tasks, and leadership roles.

Recruiters and graduate schools seek candidates who can communicate clearly, solve problems, and work in collaboration with others. These are skills you can easily develop during your college years by actively participating in group projects.

TIP **40**

KEEP METICULOUS RECORDS

"I've lost or deleted too many documents. Now I keep a hard copy of anything that's important." JING, FINANCE MAJOR

Develop a system to organize and access both printed and online documents and records.

For "hard copies," create and maintain a file of all your important academic, personal, and financial documents. You want a "paper trail" in the event that documents are needed at a later date.

Include the following in your file: grade reports, standardized test scores, class notes and handouts, canceled checks, bills, receipts, financial aid paperwork, letters of recommendation, and anything else you may need in the future.

Tip: Scan and save your most important documents online.

To avoid the possibility of loss or corruption, online and word processor documents should be organized by category and saved to a cloud file storage program such as DropBox or Google Docs.

TIP 41

STRENGTHEN YOUR **VERBAL SKILLS**

"There are two kinds of speakers. Those that are nervous and those that are liars." MARK TWAIN

Verbal communication is a valuable skill that will serve you well in college and beyond.

Speaking well is not to be confused with talking a lot. This is about quality, not quantity.

Here are a few tips:

- ▸ Watch effective speakers (in person or online) and note how they modulate and project their voice, pace their speech, exude confidence, and connect with their audiences.

- ▸ Practice speaking without unnecessary filler words (uh, like, really, ya know).

- ▸ Enroll in a public speaking class.

- ▸ Make a point of speaking up in each class.

With practice and increased confidence, you'll find that public speaking can actually be fun.

TIP **42**

LEARN
TO RELAX AND
MANAGE STRESS

*"Taking time out each day to relax
and renew is essential to living well."*
JUDITH HANSON LASATER

College stress comes at you fast—new surroundings, new people, new demands, and new expectations.

Combat physical stress with relaxation exercises, stretching, deep breathing, Yoga, Tai Chi, or meditation. Check with the Health & Wellness Program and/or Recreation Center for relaxation-related programs and offerings.

Reduce emotional stress by confiding in others—friends, family, spiritual leaders, or helping professionals at the Counseling Center. When you're stressed, it's much healthier and more effective to share your problems than it is to go it alone.

Seeking help is not an indication of weakness—it is a sign of wisdom.

TIP **43**

USE COLLEGE SUCCESS APPS AND WEBSITES

"You must accept that if the computer is a tool, it is the job of the tool user to know what to use it for." PETER DRUCKER

Productivity software and phone apps can help you be more successful—and save you time.

Go online and search for "Best Apps for College Students."

You'll find dozens of terrific programs to help you manage your time, studies, money, and more.

Here are just a few of your many options.

- ▶ Flashcards (e.g., Studies, Flashcards+)
- ▶ Study Assistance (e.g., Chegg)
- ▶ Language Translation (e.g., itranslate)
- ▶ Literature Search (e.g., Google Scholar)
- ▶ Tutorial Sites (e.g., Khan Academy, Lynda)
- ▶ Textbook Rentals (e.g., Amazon, BookRenter)
- ▶ Apps to Record Lectures (e.g., Voice Recorder)

And when you want to be entertained, inspired, and enlightened...watch TED Talks.

STRIVE FOR EXCELLENCE (NOT PERFECTION)

"Excellence is the gradual result of always striving to do better." PAT RILEY

Do you know what happens when you feel the need to be perfect?

You're constantly stressed out. You always compare yourself to others, and you feel like you're not good enough. It's as if there's a yardstick against which you compare yourself always dangling over your head.

A healthier approach involves striving for improvement, which sets you on the path to excellence.

Pat yourself on the back when you succeed, learn from your mistakes when you fall short, and accept the fact that you can't be great at everything.

You can't always be the best, but you can always strive to do your best.

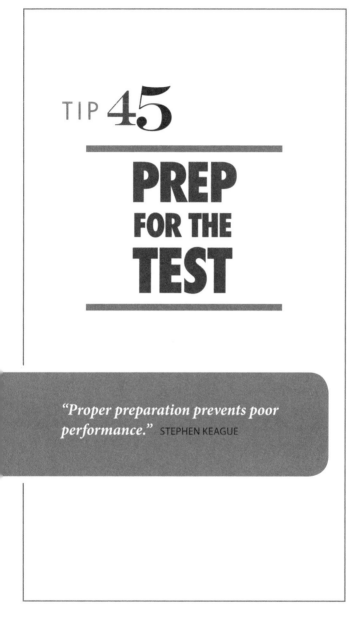

TIP **45**

PREP
FOR THE
TEST

"Proper preparation prevents poor performance." STEPHEN KEAGUE

You test well by preparing well.

- ▶ Start studying at least a week in advance.

- ▶ Actively read and reread all written materials (including your notes).

- ▶ Create flashcards.

- ▶ Quiz yourself on the material—providing answers both aloud and in writing.

- ▶ Get a good night's sleep and wake in plenty of time for a healthy breakfast.

- ▶ Arrive to class early.

- ▶ When the exam is distributed, read the instructions and review the exam in its entirety. Request clarification if necessary.

- ▶ Move on if you're stumped on a particular item. Return to it later.

- ▶ Pace yourself so you'll finish with ample time to review your answers.

After your professor returns your graded test, review the incorrect items to determine what you can do to improve future test results.

TIP **46**

CREATE
TO DO
LISTS

"Trust me—you can't just wing it in college. You need to plan out your days and create To Do lists." ALYSSA, ART MAJOR

There's a lot to keep track of in college!

Don't rely on your memory for your daily and weekly tasks— create and use a To Do list.

Keep a To Do list in your Academic Planner. Rate each item as an A (must do today), B (should do today), or C (would like to do today, but it can wait). Check off completed items and add new ones as they arise.

Your To Do list allows you to concentrate on what you need to do, instead of wasting time worrying about how you're going to get everything done, and wondering what you may have forgotten.

TAKE
ADVANTAGE
OF STUDENT SERVICES

"Once I made the effort, I found that my college offers all kinds of services."

CHRIS, EDUCATION MAJOR

Your college offers an array of services designed to keep you happy, healthy, and successful.

Participation is voluntary, so it's up to you to seek the assistance you need.

Visit your college's website for a full listing of the services available at your school. Here are a few you're likely to find.

Learning Centers – provide assistance with writing, math, and study skills

IT Help Desk – assists with technical concerns

Financial Aid – helps with scholarships, grants, and loans

And more – Counseling Center, Health Services, Recreation Center, Disability Services, and Campus Ministry

Your tuition dollars pay for these services— so why not take advantage of them?

TIP 48

LOOK FOR WAYS TO CHALLENGE YOURSELF

"If we did all the things we are capable of doing, we would literally astonish ourselves." THOMAS EDISON

Your college years are a time to broaden your horizons and take measured risks.

For example, consider doing one of these:

▸ Take an elective course on a topic of particular interest.

▸ Create a website/blog.

▸ Study abroad.

▸ Apply to the Honors program, if your GPA allows.

▸ Assume a leadership role in a campus organization.

▸ Volunteer to help a professor with his/her research.

▸ Do something you've never considered doing—tai chi, auditioning for a play, joining a political organization, or line dancing.

Go beyond your comfort zone! You will never have more opportunities within easy reach than you do right now.

TAKE PRIDE IN YOUR WORK (DON'T CHEAT)

"Honesty is the best policy. If I lose mine honor, I lose myself." SHAKESPEARE

Unfortunately, cheating occurs on every college campus.

Students submit papers done by others, copy material without proper citation, and when taking exams, use notes or copy off other students. A clear-cut violation of the academic conduct code, cheating can result in a failing grade or expulsion from school.

Students who cheat are unfair to honest students, and are ultimately cheating themselves.

Don't subvert the value of your hard-earned college education through dishonesty and shortcuts. You will derive far greater satisfaction through hard work and perseverance—qualities that will serve you well throughout your lifetime.

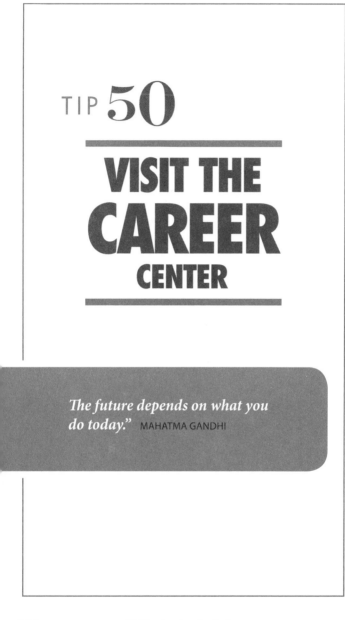

TIP **50**

VISIT THE CAREER CENTER

The future depends on what you do today." MAHATMA GANDHI

Take advantage of all the services and resources your Career Center offers.

Schedule an appointment with a career counselor as early in your college career as possible. Their services may include:

- ▸ inventories to help you identify your career interests, values, and skills

- ▸ assistance selecting majors and minors

- ▸ advice regarding internships, part-time jobs, and other activities that will enhance your career prospects

- ▸ readings, websites, and "shadowing opportunities" to acquaint you with various careers of interest

- ▸ planning for admission to graduate or professional school

- ▸ help with writing resumes, cover letters, and graduate school applications

Your Career Center helps you examine and pursue what is meaningful and valuable in your life – today and in years to come.

TIP 51

PLAN YOUR SUMMERS WELL IN ADVANCE

"By failing to prepare, you are preparing to fail." BENJAMIN FRANKLIN

To make the most of your summers, consider the following:

Take summer courses
Taking one or two courses at a nearby college is a great way to pick up some extra credits. Just make sure to confirm with your Academic Advisor that they'll transfer.

Participate in community service
Check with your college's Service Learning Office about summer volunteer opportunities.

Get an internship or job
Visit Career Services in October/November to discuss summer internships, or contact local businesses in January/February regarding summer jobs.

Don't wait until April or later to plan your summer—courses, jobs, internships, and volunteer opportunities may be long gone by then.

51 TIP REVIEW

Check off any item that you need to do, or want to work on. Let these checkmarks be a reminder of what you can do to increase your academic success.

- [ ] TIP 1   Attend All Classes
- [ ] TIP 2   Sit Up Front in Class
- [ ] TIP 3   Make the Most of Your Study Time
- [ ] TIP 4   Meet with Your Academic Advisor
- [ ] TIP 5   Complete Assignments Early
- [ ] TIP 6   Get Enough Sleep
- [ ] TIP 7   Always Follow Directions
- [ ] TIP 8   Strengthen Your Computer Skills
- [ ] TIP 9   Use an Academic Planner
- [ ] TIP 10   Actively Participate in Class
- [ ] TIP 11   Enroll in UNIV 101/First Year Courses
- [ ] TIP 12   Use Waiting Times
- [ ] TIP 13   Seek Academic Help
- [ ] TIP 14   Ace the Easy Classes

- [ ] TIP 34 Get to Know Your Professors
- [ ] TIP 35 Stay Busy But Not Overwhelmed
- [ ] TIP 36 Study According to Your Learning Style
- [ ] TIP 37 Determine Course Load Based on Difficulty
- [ ] TIP 38 Take Organized Notes
- [ ] TIP 39 Be a Good Group Member
- [ ] TIP 40 Keep Meticulous Records
- [ ] TIP 41 Strengthen Your Verbal Skills
- [ ] TIP 42 Learn to Relax and Manage Stress
- [ ] TIP 43 Use College Success Apps and Websites
- [ ] TIP 44 Strive for Excellence (Not Perfection)
- [ ] TIP 45 Prep for the Test
- [ ] TIP 46 Create To Do Lists
- [ ] TIP 47 Take Advantage of Student Services
- [ ] TIP 48 Look for Ways to Challenge Yourself
- [ ] TIP 49 Take Pride in Your Work (Don't Cheat)
- [ ] TIP 50 Visit the Career Center
- [ ] TIP 51 Plan Your Summers Well in Advance

> *"What lies behind us, and what lies before us, are tiny matters compared to what lies within us."*

Ralph Waldo Emerson

About the Authors

Alan Farber, Ph.D. has been employed in the field of college student development for 30 years. He was an Associate Director at the University of San Diego, and the Assistant Director of Career Services at Northern Illinois University (NIU). He is a writer, freelance career coach, and speaker.

Dr. Farber completed his Ph.D. in Counseling at Michigan State University. He has a Master's degree in Counseling from Ball State University and a B.A. in Psychology from Marietta College.

Linda O'Brien has written 30 booklets for students and parents—over 20 million copies have been sold to schools and colleges throughout the U.S. She worked as a counselor for 25 years and is the founder and president of Woodburn Press.

Ms. O'Brien received a Master's degree in Guidance and Counseling from Xavier University and a B.S. in Education from Miami University.